Nancy
from
Barb

D0467439

Max Ellison

The Underbark

MAX ELLISON

Published by
CONWAY HOUSE
Conway, Mich. 49722

First edition — *Sixth printing*

Printed in the United States of America

FOREWORD

We met by chance, this man
and I.
He looking, seeking, straining
to communicate and finding
few who cared to listen. I listened
and found pleasure in his words.
Now they will listen because the words are embalmed
on paper, and the voice can return to creating
sounds not meant for printer's ink.

William Curtis, Ph.D.
University of Iowa.

Dedicated to
Charlie

I know where an old beech tree
Hid a secret once for me.
Initials carved within a heart
Deep into the under-bark.
Time has healed the jack-knife scar,
But I still know where they are.

A CONSTELLATION OF TWO STARS

Two drops of molten fire
Falling through the sky
Called "Horse and Rider"
Or in days of old "Test
Star" for the eye.

I use "Horse and Rider"
When thinking from the
Heart
Or "Test Star" when my eye
Trys to keep the two apart.

With "Test Star" I am not
Testing my right to see,
But testing the faith
That binds man's heart
To the infinite of eternity.

THE GIVING

Who gives this woman to be wed?
Her mother and I.
We gave her dawn.
We gave her grace.
We stamped our image
On her face.
We gave her books,
And through the years
We calmed her early
Childhood fears.
We gave her faith.
We gave her prayer.
She walked our road.
She climbed our stairs.
And now in solemn troth
We swear,
We can not give.
We only share.

WHILE IN THE WOODS

Wanting my son to feel the moods
I had often felt while in the woods,
We camped beneath a spruce.
A black spruce, I believe,
Much taller than its neighbor trees.

High above a wind complained.
Of us I thought. It may have been rain
The wind quarreled with. I don't know.
They both left, and a little star
Watched us while we slept.

LEWIS ROY KIRBY
November 19, 1966 — Viet Nam

His war torn form we return to your arms
Gently, oh gently, hill of earth.
On this plane of prince and king,
Let the winds speak his worth.
Let the great constellations of the sky
Be his companions through the night.
Make some dream of man worth
The price of his fight.

NEVADA LARRY ELLISON
October 5, 1967 — Viet Nam

Mark him down as cannon fodder.
Mark him down as a number put out
By the war department each week.
Mark him down as carrion in a rice paddy —
A broken, twisted something that isn't
Any longer what it was.

Roll the dice again.
Turn over another card.
Flip a coin.
Draw the short straw.
My dear Mrs. Bixby.

Fate has become like a six-toed bitch.
The moon is down early.
The stars are quiet
And forever.

A leaf fell in Arlington
In Vermont a tear,
And on the plains an old man
Heard a bugle blow and said,
"What's that?"
"John's dead."
"The President?"
"Yes. He's dead."

In Plymouth they tolled a bell
While people gathered at the church to pray,
And an old man heard the bell and asked,
"What's that?"
"It's America —
Tolling a bell for John.
He's dead."
All over America a fall wind whispered,
"He's dead.
John's dead.
The President."

Henry is my friend.
He's old now, bent
And around the temples grey.
Holds his head sideways
As if listening.
I asked him once what he heard.
Henry couldn't say if anything.
Just a habit, I suppose, or a favor
To some lameness he might know.

Henry's grandfather was a slave
Who plowed cotton with a mule.
Once while he was plowing,
Henry told me this,
He heard thunder and thought a storm
Was coming from the old log meeting house.
Shiloh was only five miles away.
But someone said it wasn't storm but cannon,
And there was word that men were fighting.

Henry's grandfather left the mule,
Young cotton plants and the rule
About master and slave in the field that day,
And towards the old log meeting house
Made his way, listening
To the thunder of cannon.

Henry's old now.
He holds his head a little sideways
As if listening.
I ask him what he hears.
He doesn't know.

AMERICA

America's destiny was bought with blood.
Shiloh thunder, New Guinea mud,
Winds on the prairie, a buffalo track,
The smoke of Pittsburgh and away, way back
I see shadows — shadows of men —

John Brown

Lincoln

Paine and Clay

Appomattox Court House, an old man in grey,
Heavy artillery massed on the Marne,
A camp meeting prayer, an unpainted barn.
All this is America.

I see mountains and valleys, rivers in flood,
The tomb of a soldier unknown but to God.
I see ships at their mooring, a moon on the wane,
A city at dawning, an old country lane,
And I whisper, "America."

I thrill at the shadows cast by big men.
Listen their words! Hear them again!
"I have but the one lamp by which my feet are guided."
"Don't give up the ship."
"We have just begun to fight."

"Saw sub — sank same."
"I speak today not as the Senator from Massachusetts."
"The only terms of surrender I will accept are unconditional."
"I regret that I have but the one life to give."
"Shoot if you must this old grey head,
    but spare your country's flag."
"That these dead shall not have died in vain."
And in world war one the sergeant yelling
As he went over the top, "Come on boys, what the hell!
Do you want to live forever?"
That was America talking.

The dreams of America are held in the arms
Of a mother with babe. It's found on the farms,
In a factory at midnight, A wind by the sea.
Dreams of America! They whisper to me!
"Do you know what I am going to be when I get big?"
"We are going to try."
"He graduates next June."
"We named him after his Grandfather."
"There's quite a building program going on at the University."
And some guy jerks the lever of a one armed bandit at Reno
And gets two bars and a lemon.
That's America — dreaming.

Where are the soldiers buried?
In a grove of trees at Vicksburg
I saw their graves on a hillside,
Neat rows of government issue stones
Noting their name and regiment,
Or marking them down "Unknown."

I have seen in township graveyards
their flag — as if marking the spot
As a place where an eagle fell,
Bringing down glory and thunder
To this last spot where they dwell.
Where are the soldiers buried?

I stood on a hill in Kentucky
Listing their names on my mind;
A volunteer battalion from Ohio,
The Second Brigade, Tennessee,
A soldier named Smith, 10th Michigan.
There were ten in a row listed only by name,
Their regiment and state unknown.
Whether blue or grey, I couldn't know.
Where are the soldiers buried?
Arlington, Flander's Field,
A green grassy bank on the Marne.
Strange stars — strange lands.
And I know a farm where a soldier's grave
Plowed over, neglected, forgot.
And sometimes at night the thunder rolls low.
Where are the soldiers buried?

SHILOH SOLDIER

I stood beside a soldier's grave,
A Shiloh and Battle of the Wilderness soldier's grave
Who was buried on our farm.
A maple tree, a shaft of stone, a barefoot boy,
We three alone by the soldier's grave,
A Strawberry Plains soldier's grave,
Buried on our farm.

I had wildflowers in a jar.
Grandma couldn't walk that far
And asked if I could leave my game
Of playing cowboy in the lane
And take them to the soldier's grave,
The war soldier's grave,
Who was buried on our farm.

I placed flowers by the stone,
Then crossed my heart and felt alone.
For deep inside I wondered why
A Shiloh soldier had to die,
A Battle of the Wilderness soldier,
A Strawberry Plains soldier,
Had to die and be buried on our farm.

THE BRONZE HORSE

To you who made the mold, and cast
From fire the molten bronze,
You must have known the thunder of his hoofs
To have captured this splendor I view.
Around his eye still lingers some flame
Uncooled from life or fire, and his mane,
Unruffled by the breeze, reflects the sun.
In fancy I can hear him as he runs among the stars.
The barns are gone. The fields are not the same.
There are new records — new names.
Racing silks flecked with foam,
And from the head of the stretch I hear thunder
As he starts for home, and old Mr. Will saying,
"He was the mostest horse!" All this in bronze.
And I hear thunder.

I saw a herd of bicycles
Resting by the school house,
All with wide spread silver antlers.
Some were standing.
Some were lying down
With heads half turned
And antlers pointing downward.
Soon will come a host of youthful cowpokes
To start the stampede.

I SAW THE BRIDGE

My friend traveled a thousand miles to see a bridge.
I spent an hour searching for an oriole's nest,
And found the ribbon black skin that a snake had shed,
A vixen's pup dead from a punctured throat,
And, in the summer dust, a weasel track.
My friend came back and said,
"I saw the bridge."

GOING OUT

In an old house I made ready for the night.
Listened to the wind who must have thought me deaf,
Watched the ballerina dancing of a candle flame,
Unlaced what tensions day had left.
Took down a tangled dream from time's old shelf,
Then watched a cloud part, so the moon could step inside
And see a man, a candle, and a doom.

I'll walk through the towns calling Noah,
Knowing where you are, but
Seeking the beginning of that
Which ended long before I knew.
Noah —Noah — Noah.
I'll walk through the towns calling Noah.
I'll walk through the streets calling you.

We buried my artist friend today,
Buried him on a high hill
Without benefit of clergy
Or talk of a house with many mansions.

We gave him back to the earth —
Left him in the arms of a mother
Who had nursed the trees and animals
He loved to paint.

We left him in the shadow of a juniper,
And knew that the wind would come,
While the stars would run their course.
And the universe, hardly knowing
Of his passing and passion,
Would be the same.

The rain would come.
The grass would dry in the summer.
The night would murmur sounds he could not hear.
Please — No tears. He had finished.
The picture was dry.
The colors had set.

A ladder well could serve my need for outer space.
Braced well with roof and ground,
Like some four-footed beast I could reach the peak
To take one anxious look around.
And, if not liking what I saw,
Or unwilling to take my leave,
I would have something solid on my side
To bring me well below the perigee of eaves.

The Inglee bird is extinct I guess.
At least I never find their nest,
And the woods in summer never ring
With the kind of song the Inglee sings.
You say there never was such bird?
But in grade three I read this line,
"Inglee birds sing all the time."
They're extinct now, so never mind.

Marnie's back to school.
No fan fare,
Just the dawn a-peeking,
A headlight, and she's gone.

The swooping owl nicked the glare
My headlights made as I drove where
A half filled swale of elder brush
Hid rabbit tracks.
A flash of brown, some under white,
An instant caught within my sight,
And when the night had claimed him back,
I drove on.

I stood in the reptile house
Close by the cage of the adder.
The plate read, "African Puff Adder — Poisonous."
Fascinated by its beauty of motion,
I was reminded of you:
Motion that flowed and was silent,
Motion that captured the beauty of movement and rhythm
And flowed like words through my being.
The kiss of either would be fatal.

Beyond my ken or sight
And hid among the shadows of the night
Learned men with glass can spy,
A million light years from the eye,
Galaxies.

While on this earth path where I've trod,
I ask and receive as answer, only God.
But this I know. There is some light
From stars that burned a million years ago.

LINES WRITTEN IN MEMORY OF A NEIGHBOR

A simple man, they said, was he.
But he knew how to chop a tree
To make it fall just where he wished.
Is being simple such as this?
The way of summer, bird and nest.
His days were toil. His nights were rest.
And now in death beneath the sod,
Unknown to man — perhaps to God.

The earth holds many secrets not meant for me to solve.
I picked a flower once from wooded noon,
But knew not why it chose a shaded spot,
Or how it made a yellow with its bloom.
I only knew the beauty of its face.
I remember that I saved the flower to press
Between the pages of a book that spoke of love
And hinted at a something after death.

HINTS OF SPRING

Last night I heard an owl
Hoot a lovesong to the night.
No answer came, but I am sure it will.
And then I saw a waning moon
Rise just before the dawn
To look down on my fields so dark and still.

I've caught other hints of spring
In a streak of living red
That chased a herd of shadows from my woods,
And a little shaft of morning
That came dancing down the hill
And started romancing with some buds.

I saw the resurrection in a daffodil.
There was no cross nor cry of pain,
But a wind from March, a splash of rain,
And there arose from winter's tomb
The ribbon leaves and yellow bloom of a daffodil.

APRIL RAIN

The limbs show shiny wet and cold.
The sky and bark are one in grey.
A little bird hunched on a twig
Waits patiently a better day.
Quite unprotected from the rain,
In silence waits the day to clear,
While unequipped to trade for grief
The beauty of a tiny tear.

TRYSTING SONG

I meant to gravel pack the hole
Where rain and moonlight
Made a pool for toads,
A trysting place for warty love
And angled songs to float above
Where I, though bowed with heavy load,
Am thrilled to hear the song of toads.

Old Bob's been dead for forty years
But apple trees still bloom,
Mostly just for worm and bee
Or some old duff that limps, like me,
Back to the place where his house stood
Against a hill of maple wood,
To rest on it's foundation stone
While mem'ry wanders back alone.
Forty years Bob's been away,
But his trees are wild with bloom today.

RUNAWAY HOLLYHOCKS
for Veloise

Two hollyhocks that I saw stood
Knee deep in grass beside a woods.
Hand in hand they seemed to say,
"Just look at us! We've run away!"

I've seen hollyhocks before
Standing by some country door,
Curtsying shadows in the lane,
Peeking in some kitchen pane,
Or doing sentry by the gate,
But these were lost, and it was late.

I can't believe that any fiend
Would turn them out, or be so mean
As when they bloomed to come and say,
"We don't want hollyhocks today."

I think, perhaps, some love instead,
For one was white, and one was red,
Caused them through the night to say,
"When morning comes, we'll run away."

Shy warbler who sings to me from leafy shade,
Although my eyes look high to see,
It's by your song alone I know you,
And you know less than that of me.

I'm quite content to leave it as we have it.
We'll share the tree and summer, but
Your song will be the one we put our faith in.
The ones I know sometimes have proven wrong.

RED TAILED HAWK

I envy you who rides upon the wind
And neighbors equally with cloud and tree,
Who presses wings against an August sky
While scanning fields where needs that I must be.

THE INCHWORM

A little worm was lost on me.
I didn't know his breed or clan
But saw him in the fading light
Wandering lonely on my hand.

Caught down from leaf or up from grass,
His body bathed in greenish tones,
I guessed an eyelash for his length,
And wondered if he sought some home.

His inching body moved through hair
As tall as trees that I could know,
As if he searched for some hard fact—
A little thought a worm must know.

I raised my hand high to my eye
And lined him with the tip of pine,
But knew the distance was too far
To reach down to his worm-like mind.

Beyond the pine an evening star—
A little gasp of purple light
Flickering in the early dark
With a hundred tongues to lick the night.

Beyond the star I too must inch
And search for facts my mind can't learn.
To what, and where, and out beyond—
I grope and reach just like the worm.

A tall hollyhock
Bowed with the wind,
Peeked at my window,
Straightened again,
Stood close by the house
Not blocking a view,
But peeked in again
When the wind blew.

So, all through the day
It's been peek-a-boo hour,
I with a book,
The wind with a flower,
I with a thought, but
The wind, I can see,
Is telling the flowers
To keep watch of me.

I stopped once where a wild rose grew
From seed, I suppose. I only knew
It grew along a road where no one lived
And had no reason to be there.
But reason is not needed for a rose.

Its three petal blooms were safe from vase.
The rose was terrible with its thorns,
And grew alone beside a road
Where no one lived.

The scarlet tanager I saw upon the dunes
Was like a ruby melting in the sun.
The music of his song flung from a wind bent pine
Was only to remind me they were his dunes. Not mine.

There is nothing left of summer
But the green of the new seeding,
A bottle half filled with sun tan lotion,
And some place on the lawn
A croquet mallet that wasn't put away.
A few crudely lettered "U PICK" signs
Along the highway remind me
That once was harvest, where now
Is just a blotch of brown and grey.

OCTOBER

The year has lived too long to be bound
By inhibitions and conventions.
October, you are like a painted woman,
And I love you.
Splash in your vermillion paint pot if you wish,
Or turn me your cold shoulder.
Kiss me with warmth.
Powder your cheeks with white.
Wear a scarlet gown,
Or stand naked under a hunter's moon
With your yellow hair falling over your shoulders.
I'll love you forever, October.

CATCH DOWN THE WIND

Catch down the wind.
Unhook it from its tangle in the trees.
Perhaps it searched for leaves,
But they have gone.
Some partridge hunters came, and when they left,
The trees were bare.

It may have been the frost.
I do not know the cause or where.
The wind is lonesome now.
I hear it crying somewhere in the trees.
And starlight's drifting low along the hill.
Catch down the wind and walk with me.

WINTER NIGHT'S WALK

In a hushed and silent night of trees
A spread of white lies waiting for my tracks,
And above the bare branches, points of light
To mark or guide, should I come back.
Deep in the woods I stand and share no sound,
Unless perhaps some old and creaking tree
Complains against the winter and the night,
And drops a shower of frost stars down on me.

TO A WHITE OWL

Welcome!
There isn't much moon left,
And my fields lie glazed and blue
With little leering drifts
Close by each post and tree.
But you are welcome to hunt.

Rabbits?
Yes, there are rabbits.
I have seen their tracks along the hill,
But I must go home and rest
And will not hear their shrill cry.

Tomorrow,
While in some hollow tree
You dream of open tundras,
I'll hunt — it's about the same.
Only, unlike you soaring softly there above,
I must be down in the very middle
Of that which I can't love.

The winter night
Doth ram the wind
Against my bones.
The flame grows dim,
Until a spark
Is left alone
To deal with dark.
A tiny spark,
It well may be
My soul's one link
With eternity.

SNOW FENCE

I built a fence — a fence for the wind.
I neither planned to stop it long
Nor fence it in from its night time wandering.
My thoughts were this —
If she is bent on such mischief as drifting snow,
Why not pile it here along the hill
Instead of on a road where I must go.
So I built a fence — a fence for the wind.

Six hundred crates and boxes in a row
Were piled along a hillside path
Where she must go to reach my road.
With six hundred crates and boxes
I built a fence — a fence for the wind.

And then, when all the skies were fair,
With a million snowflakes in her hair,
She came dancing through the night.
She kissed the willow tree in passing,
Took the lane,
Came down across another field to fill my road.
She never even saw the fence I had built —
A fence for the wind.

Somewhere — out past yesterday —
I heard your voice.
Some small thing you said
That escaped me at the time.
But memory is a strange bedfellow,
And I must share tomorrow with
Some dreams that once were yours and mine.

The moon hangs low. It's in the fulling.
I found a skin of ice before
The horses came to drink.
This morning I remembered
Something you once said.
It was out past yesterday,
But I recalled — and it was nice.

I carved a name. I carved a day.
It was my thought and way of saying goodbye.
I left while the sun was starting
Its lonely journey across the sky,
Knowing that I might never come back.
And yet part of me must stay
Forever among the dunes.
I carved a name. I felt the grief of leaving.
While the lighthouse lost its sweeping beam in dawn,
I carved a day, and I was gone.

THE ROAD TO ORMOC

You were lying there broken and twisted,
Littered with the backwash of battle,
Smelling of men who were rotten,
And looking like a banquet board
Where death had just feasted.

I cursed through that long night of darkness!
Cursed that I should lie in the Ormoc
Listening to death do her singing,
Singing a song with a machine gun
With artillery playing the bass part.

He fell
Half in the water,
Half on the beach,
And the outgoing tide
Pulled at his feet and legs,
While his eyes
Became fixed upon nothing
And were glazed.

For awhile
The tide and the beach struggled
Over who was to have him.
The tide won,
And gently pulled him
Out in the water,
And his fatigue jacket
Ballooned up like a sail.

The company clerk wrote,
"Missing in Action."

STRONG TIMBERS

Strong timbers,
That bend well in the storm
And take the wind with ease and free,
I have seen your line against the dark of hills
Marking a guide for me
Throughout the night of fear and hate.

Strong timbers,
While thunders roamed the sky,
I thought I saw you give beneath the storm and cried.
But where death whistled high above,
There was a flash of dawn,
And I could see against the hill,
Still standing — strong timbers.

TICKET HOME

His face was white
As the bandages
That bound his stomach.
His damp, red hair
Still showed a ring
Pressed there by his helmet liner.

His smile was wide
And genuine
As he told me
Some damned Nip
Had given him
A ticket back to the States.

He wanted a smoke.
I gave him
One that was lit,
But some medic called,
"He just came back from surgery,
And can't smoke."

I took it back
From a still hand
Lying across
A shattered stomach.
So quickly he died.

THE OUTPOST

Where darkness hides the day along the hill,
He sits with lonesomeness and still a memory,
One or two perhaps of what the day had brought
Back in the past, remembered now with sadness.

Along the ridge darkness
Has pressed his comrades down in sleep
Below the surface of the ground
Where he must keep the watch.

To watch or not be found he doesn't know.
The answer puzzles him, but not for long,
For there's a shadow stretched out on the ground
Where night and tree have met.

And yet!
It seems to move!
Should he awaken some one else to see,
Or trust it's just the shadow of a tree?

Until the moon decides for him,
His hand strokes rifle gently,
While with finger back
He finds the safety guard.

The night moves softly,
And shadows
Stretch out on the ground
While he guards.

56

Alone will be the password.
Death will keep the watch.
And no tomorrow promised for the guard.
The night will sit so lonely by his side,
He'll wonder why she's wrapped in just a rainshroud
Stained with blood.

His tiny hour
Of blaze and story,
His path to fame,
His road to glory
Ended
On a field where blood
Made the soil red.
And dead,
With locked eyes
Looking
Toward the sky,
He received
No answer.

This hand so dead,
With quiet bones around
The red rust of
A silent gun,
Cover it
With earth and the dearth
Of thoughts
That man once held true.
Cover it
With a small sprinkling
From the dust of time.
Cover it from the eye,
And let the grim
Sockets of its skull
Lie forever
Looking upward.

THE ARMISTICE

Where hangs some mark of hell upon a hill
Strong trees once grew,
And today splintered stubs are hid by mist.
Tomorrow — if tomorrow — the mist will go,
And where the ground is red and moist
New shoots will show.

HONORED GLORY

or

Unknown soldier talks back to guard.

You who mark my sleep with measured tred,
Remember that my name,
My beginning,
My end,
My fame
Is unknown,
And my sleep can only be marked by infinity,
And not by your measured tred through the ages.

WISH STAR

Above the hill,
Beneath the pine,
She shyly appears
To take my wish
As calling card,
Then disappears.

STOVER SPRING

I stopped by a spring,
A flowing place,
With a stone basin
To catch my face.
On a tree by it's side
Hung an old tin cup —
A cup that was empty
And should be filled up.
Put there by one, though
A stranger to me,
Was willing to share
His spring and his tree
With a man whose ways
Were devious at best
And had stopped on the edge
Of the night for a rest,
For a drinking of springs,
For a sorting of thoughts,
For a knowing of where
We are on a walk.

SUCCESS

I've learned to say my name, and speak
The year, the month, the day of week,
Please and Thanks with some small grace,
To know myself within the race
Of human beings where I walk.
I've learned to read, to write, to talk,
To cipher numbers one to ten.
I drop them there and start again.
I've learned the quiet of an hour.
I've learned the beauty of a flower.

SELF PORTRAIT

I stood under the night and heard
The stars call my name.
Later I confirmed it where
The brook made a pool to reflect
Their glory and the face of a fool.

I'LL WAIT FOR THE MOON

I'll wait for the moon
And still have time to get home.
It will not matter if I am late
And supper is over. They'll leave a plate.

For it's when I think of that ride alone
From the place I work to the place I home,
A lonesomeness comes around my heart.
I'll wait for the moon.

I'll wait for the moon
And still have time to get home.
There is more work, and I'm not through
With a couple of thoughts I had of you.
Supper can wait, and I can too.
I'll wait for the moon.

OXEN SONG

Some boyhood memory calls him back.
I almost see him now
Who farmed the forty next to ours
With oxen and a plow.
No reins to guide those yoked up beasts,
Old Scott would plod along,
And when he wanted them to haw
He called out with a song.

"Teedle dum dum dum
Teedle dum dum dum
Give me the haw, God damn you,
Give me the haw."

I have watched him in the morning sun
Stripe up a field with plow.
Or caught him coming down the road
With those patient son's of cows,
While Scott sat high up on the seat
A–looking down at me,
And calling out his oxen song
And singing for the "Gee".

Memory keeps on egging me
To get back there again,
And stand up close beside the fence
Where evening's coming in,
To listen for old Scott to sing.
I'd hear him, that I know,
Singing down through forty years
And calling for the "Whoa."

This was a field.
You wouldn't know it now,
For there is underbrush and woods
Where once the plow.
And I remember when corn stood
Against an August sky.
But now the leaves are dead and bitter
From too much living.
A small snake crawls in search of sleep
Or perhaps some warmth that isn't there.

Some rinds of humanity
That time has squeezed and left,
An obscenity written on the wall,
Some crumbs of death remain.
And who will sweep away this naked silence,
Or call some child to a wall to show
The black stains where once an ivy grew?

The sun goes down, and night
Walks a silent beat.
While down-cast eyes never notice
The fullness of the moon crossing
Their dismal canyon of a street.

EMPTY UNIVERSE

While stars burst
And galaxies exploded their way
Into a silent sea of space,
This small speck of Cosmic dust
Cooled,
Formed its mountains,
Then a million years of steady rain
To fill the sea.
Yesterday a plant appeared.
This morning there was me.

JOHN ROGERS

The human life
Comes in assorted shapes
And sizes.
The one old John wore
Was the large
Ninety-eight.
He wore it
Through the town with
Price tag showing,
Long beard,
Blue eyes,
And white hair blowing.

Go back, my son,
To the sea and sky
Where the gulls wheel,
Where the winds cry,
Where the high surf keeps rolling in.
Go back —
Go back!

Go back, my lad,
To the stars and the sea,
Back to the tides and the foam,
Back to the breast of the loving sea,
Back —
To the sailor's home.

The sea remembers our face as
Some form of life she tossed on her shores
Too many times, until at last,
By some divine truth, or
By evoking the laws of evolution,
We grew legs and crawled away
From the ocean to this place in time
Where we are resting momentarily,
While we reach for a star.

After
The leaves have fallen
And the flowers are dead,
We will sell the house,
Take down the beds,
Remove the pictures from the wall,
Pack books,
Wrap each glass in paper,
Pull up our roots,
List our regrets,
Burn paper,
Carry out old cans,
Then,
Tempted and lonesome,
Wait for the van.

In the market place of time
I bartered thought for truth.
The old merchant, a hard dealer,
Often gave me compromise for change.
Such coin I accepted with loathing,
But used it in some bargains I have made.

This place in time
Is all I know.
Behind is past,
Ahead is go,
Eternities both
With me between.
This slice I know
Is thin and lean.
This place in time
Is little more
Than what it takes
To close a door,
The sharpest note
A cricket sings,
The flicking of
A wild bird's wing.
I'll not regret
That left behind.
What lies ahead
I will not mind.

I too must die.
Like a spear of grass I will wither to the ground,
To share "Forever" with a sky and hill,
To hear the night fill with wind,
With no rain or sun to revive my bones.
And the unsprouted seed from my tumble-weed soul
Will lie in the dust, alone.

I too must die.
I will become a kinsman to the wind,
Drift as dust in the breath of a prairie fire,
Be tossed by a mountain storm,
Know the lonesomeness of time,
Drift with a deep tide, going out
But never in.
I too must die.

There is no sound on the hill, only wind.
There is no cover but the sky,
And at night a patchwork quilt of stars
For those who die.
Love walks a quiet path a little while.
Summer stands a minute, breathless before she goes.
There is no sound on the hill, only wind.

In single file my brain has set
A list of things I'll not forget;
A sudden rain on roof of barn,
The greyness on the bark of beech,
Some cowbells heard through morning fog,
The barking of a country dog that knew no fright,
And yet must talk back with the night.
I'll not forget the wood smoke smell of pine
That kindled well the morning fire,
Or the cow barn when the hay was new.
I'll not forget the thrill of love,

or you.